MATH GAMES GRADE 5

By
JOYCE A. STULGIS-BLALOCK

COPYRIGHT © 2004 Mark Twain Media, Inc.

ISBN 1-58037-274-0

Printing No. CD-404001

Mark Twain Media, Inc., Publishers
Distributed by Carson-Dellosa Publishing Company, Inc.

HPS 232443

Table of Contents

Introduction to the Teacher

These math games were developed over the past several years. Students in many grade levels have tried them and have really enjoyed playing them. The games were designed to reinforce the National Council of Teachers of Mathematics (NCTM) Standards. The standards that pertain to each game are noted at the top of each page.

The games are unique, because they incorporate several skills. They are intended to be played without paper and pencil to enable students to exercise mental math skills; however, with some of the pages, students may need paper and pencil. They are not only math "skills" games, but are also games of "strategy." The students must have good math knowledge, but they must also be thinking of where they want to move in the answer boxes with their next solution to achieve three boxes in a row. (*Note:* Each game takes about 5 to 15 minutes to play individually or as teams or 10 to 20 minutes as a class.)

Here are some ways in which the games may be played:
1. Students can be given a page as a morning practice sheet.
2. They can play the games as a race, to see who finishes first.
3. The pages can be used as test preparation.
4. They can be played with partners or in teams of three.
5. If the teacher makes a transparency of a game, it can be played with competing teams within the class.
   (*More detailed directions follow this page.*)

I hope this book will help you and your students.

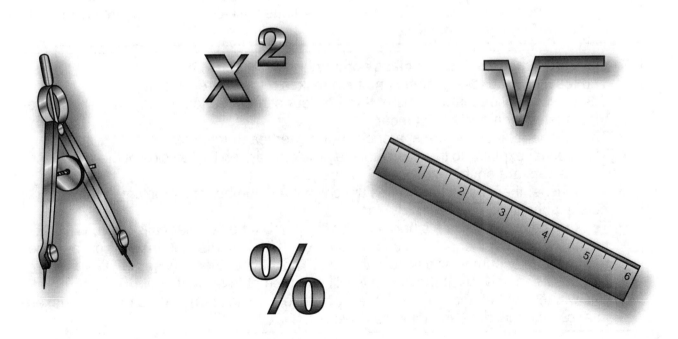

Directions for Playing Math Games

To play the games individually as a review, a learning exercise, or as a morning warm-up exercise:
1. First, the teacher chooses the skill he/she wants the students to practice.
2. Copies of the chosen game are made for each student.
3. The games are passed out facedown on the students' desks.
4. When the teacher says, "Go," the students turn over the game, and they begin to match answers in the boxes on the right side of the page to the problems listed on the left side of the page.
5. They write the number of the problem in the box that has the correct answer. They must then cross out the problem they have solved. When the whole class has finished, the teacher calls out the answers, and the students correct their own work, or they can exchange with a partner, and the partner can correct the game.

To play the games in teams of 2 or 3 players:
1. The teacher chooses the game with the skills the students need to practice.
2. Copies of the chosen game are made for every two or three students.
3. The class is divided into teams of two or three students, and it is determined who will go first, second, and third.
4. The teacher passes out the games facedown, one game per team.
5. When the teacher says, "Go," the students turn over the game.
6. The student who goes first chooses any problem on the left side of the page to complete. If the answer is correct, or the other player(s) agree with the answer, the first player puts his/her initials in the answer box and crosses out the question. If the answer is NOT correct, that student loses a turn. Right or wrong, the game paper passes to student number two. After student number two finishes, the game passes to student number three, and so the game continues.
7. The person who gets any three answer boxes in a row wins. Each answer box can only be used one time for a win. The game can continue until all of the boxes are claimed or until a win is no longer possible.

To play the games as a whole-class activity:
1. The teacher chooses the game and then makes a transparency of it.
2. The class is divided into teams of three or four students each. Each team should be represented by a name or number.
3. The teacher places the transparency on the overhead projector.
4. The teacher explains to the class that the problems are on the left side of the page, and the answers are on the right side of the page.
5. The teacher then states that he/she will call out the number of a problem; for example, he/she announces: "Number 5."
6. The first person to raise his/her hand, or the person the teacher calls upon, will state the answer to Number 5. If it is correct, then that team claims that answer box, and the team's name or number is placed in that box. The teacher then crosses out the problem that has been solved, so the students will not attempt to solve it again.
7. The winner is either the team with the most boxes, or the team that claims three boxes in a row; the teacher can make the choice.

NCTM Standard: Number and Operations – understand relationships among numbers

Hook Some Patterns

Determine the number that completes each pattern below, and find the answer in the boxes to the right.

37	-21	19	5
45	15	6	2
25	-9	7	21
39	11	48	-22

1. 5, 10, 15, 20, _____
2. 3, 6, 9, 12, _____
3. 9, 8, 7, 6, _____
4. 32, 36, 40, 44, _____
5. 31, 33, 35, 37, _____
6. 35, 36, 38, 41, _____
7. 35, 39, 36, 40, _____
8. -1, -3, -5, -7, _____
9. -1, +2, +5, +8, _____
10. 3, 5, 4, 6, 5, _____
11. 33, 30, 27, 24, _____
12. 42, 33, 24, 15, _____
13. -7, -9, -12, -16, _____
14. -2, -7, -12, -17, _____
15. 5, 10, 14, 17, _____
16. 28, 20, 13, 7, _____

3

NCTM Standard: Algebra – use symbolic algebra to represent problems

NAB AN EXPRESSION

Match each algebraic expression below with an equation in the boxes to the right.

n + 6	*n* + 3	*n* ÷ 4	*n* - 6
5 ÷ *n*	15 ÷ *n*	6 - *n*	6*n*
n ÷ 6	6 + *n*	3 - *n*	*n* ÷ 5
5*n*	3 + *n*	3*n*	4 ÷ *n*

1. *n* more than the quantity six
2. the quantity fifteen divided by *n*
3. six more than the quantity *n*
4. the quantity five divided by *n*
5. five times the quantity *n*
6. six less than *n*
7. *n* more than the quantity three
8. *n* less than the quantity six
9. the quantity *n* divided by five
10. the quantity *n* divided by four
11. *n* divided by the quantity six
12. six times the quantity *n*
13. *n* subtracted from the quantity three
14. four divided by the quantity *n*
15. three added to the quantity *n*
16. the quantity three times *n*

NCTM Standard: Algebra – use symbolic algebra to represent problems

Peg Some Algebraic Equations

Decide the value of the unknown factor or divisor in each equation below, and find the answer in the boxes to the right.

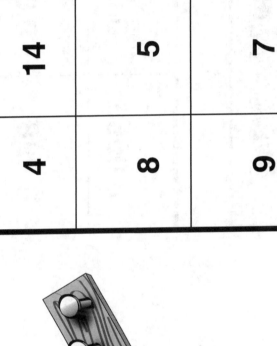

11	10	12	90
4	14	2	94
8	5	3	70
9	7	25	6

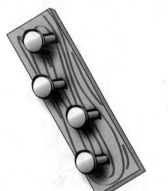

1. $55 \div n = 5$
2. $22 \times n = 88$
3. $34 \times n = 68$
4. $78 \div n = 26$
5. $96 \div n = 12$
6. $72 \div n = 6$
7. $24 \times n = 144$
8. $20 \times n = 280$
9. $27 \times n = 189$
10. $32 \times n = 160$
11. $234 \div n = 26$
12. $500 \div n = 50$
13. $420 \div n = 6$
14. $540 \div n = 6$
15. $2 \times n = 188$
16. $3 \times n = 75$

NCTM Standard: Number and Operations – compute fluently

DECIMAL DASH

Solve each of the problems below, and then find the answer in the boxes to the right.

0.0056	0.015	0.032
0.028	0.024	0.0035
0.0040	0.28	0.020
0.21	0.049	0.035
0.056	0.12	0.021

1. $0.4 \times 0.7 =$

2. $0.4 \times 0.3 =$

3. $0.4 \times 0.05 =$

4. $0.4 \times 0.07 =$

5. $0.4 \times 0.08 =$

6. $0.05 \times 0.07 =$

7. $0.05 \times 0.08 =$

8. $0.07 \times 0.08 =$

9. $0.3 \times 0.05 =$

10. $0.3 \times 0.07 =$

11. $0.3 \times 0.08 =$

12. $0.7 \times 0.3 =$

13. $0.7 \times 0.05 =$

14. $0.7 \times 0.07 =$

15. $0.7 \times 0.08 =$

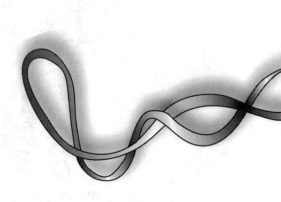

6

NCTM Standard: Number and Operations – understand ways of representing numbers and work flexibly with fractions, decimals, and percents

Drag in Decimals on a Number Line

Determine the decimal that would be at the arrow on each number line below. Find the decimal represented by the arrow in the boxes to the right.

1. 1 ——↑—— 2
2. 2 ——↑—— 3
3. 5 ——↑—— 6
4. 10 ————↑ 11
5. 15 ——↑—— 16
6. 16 ——↑—— 17
7. 0.10 ——↑—— 0.20
8. 0.10 ——↑—— 0.14
9. 20 ——↑—— 21
10. 0.20 ————↑ 0.30
11. 20 ——↑—— 21
12. 0.15 ——↑—— 0.17
13. 0.10 ——↑—— 0.12
14. 0.12 ——↑—— 0.14
15. 12 ↑———— 14

16.5	0.16	12.5
0.11	0.13	1.5
5.5	10.75	20.25
0.12	2.25	0.25
15.25	20.75	0.15

7

NCTM Standard: Number and Operations – compute fluently and make reasonable estimates

NAB A PRODUCT

Find the answers to the following problems in the boxes to the right.

1. 0.5 × 101 =
2. 2.1 × 101 =
3. 0.9 × 56 =
4. 2.1 × 121 =
5. 1.5 × 5 =
6. 0.9 × 121 =
7. 0.5 × 56 =
8. 0.9 × 5 =
9. 2.1 × 56 =
10. 1.5 × 101 =
11. 1.5 × 121 =
12. 2.1 × 5 =
13. 0.9 × 101 =
14. 1.5 × 56 =
15. 0.5 × 5 =
16. 0.5 × 121 =

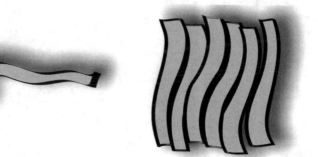

108.9	50.5	4.5	28
50.4	2.5	254.1	60.5
151.5	10.5	181.5	117.6
7.5	84	212.1	90.9

8

NCTM Standard: Number and Operations – compute fluently and make reasonable estimates

Find the answers to the following problems in the boxes to the right.

1. 0.52 x 6 =
2. 0.22 x 0.4 =
3. 0.02 x 0.42 =
4. 0.8 x 0.81 =
5. 0.5 x 0.31 =
6. 0.61 x 0.2 =
7. 0.72 x 0.2 =
8. 0.81 x 0.3 =
9. 0.61 x 0.3 =
10. 0.52 x 0.6 =
11. 0.22 x 0.04 =
12. 0.2 x 0.42 =
13. 0.08 x 0.81 =
14. 0.05 x 0.31 =
15. 0.61 x 0.02 =
16. 0.72 x 0.02 =

Pinch Decimal Multiples

0.243	0.0144	0.312	0.0155
0.648	0.122	0.088	0.183
3.12	0.144	0.0084	0.0648
0.155	0.0122	0.0088	0.084

NCTM Standard: Number and Operations – compute fluently and make reasonable estimates

SNAP UP CHANGE

If you had a twenty-dollar bill and you spent the following amounts, find the amount of change you would receive from the clerk in the boxes to the right.

$8.75	$3.75	$9.25	$9.70
$17.75	$8.90	$14.65	$14.40
$4.00	$4.75	$17.90	$13.75
$14.75	$13.65	$13.15	$15.75

1. $5 $5 $1 10¢
2. $1 $1 5¢ 5¢
3. $5 25¢
4. $5 $5 25¢ 25¢ 25¢
5. $1 $1 $1 25¢
6. $5 $1 $5 25¢
7. $5 $5 $1
8. 10¢ 10¢ 10¢ 10¢ 10¢ $5
9. $5 $1 25¢ 10¢
10. 10¢ 10¢ 10¢ $5 $5
11. $1 $5 5¢ 5¢ 5¢ 5¢ 5¢
12. $1 $5 25¢ $5 $5
13. $1 25¢ 25¢ 25¢ 10¢ $5
14. $5 $5 $5 25¢
15. $1 $1 25¢
16. $5 5¢ 5¢ 5¢ 5¢ 5¢ 5¢ 5¢ 5¢

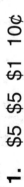

10

NCTM Standard: Number and Operations – compute fluently

Find the answers to the following problems in the boxes to the right.

0.006	0.81	0.20	0.025
0.035	0.028	0.064	0.032
0.036	0.021	0.01	0.16
0.018	0.18	0.049	0.30

Snare Decimal Multiples

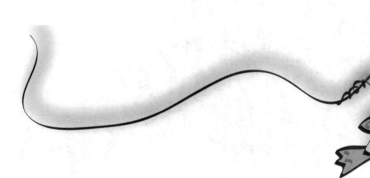

1. 0.02 x 0.3 =
2. 0.4 x 0.5 =
3. 0.07 x 0.3 =
4. 0.4 x 0.4 =
5. 0.6 x 0.5 =
6. 0.08 x 0.8 =
7. 0.9 x 0.9 =
8. 0.07 x 0.4 =
9. 0.6 x 0.03 =
10. 0.6 x 0.3 =
11. 0.5 x 0.05 =
12. 0.4 x 0.08 =
13. 0.07 x 0.7 =
14. 0.4 x 0.09 =
15. 0.05 x 0.7 =
16. 0.1 x 0.1 =

11

NCTM Standard: Number and Operations – compute fluently and make reasonable estimates

Find the answers to the following problems in the boxes to the right.

A Quotient Sprint

200	10	$3\frac{1}{6}$	$11\frac{4}{5}$
$4\frac{3}{4}$	$10\frac{5}{9}$	19	40
100	$9\frac{1}{2}$	$47\frac{1}{2}$	$6\frac{1}{3}$
15	59	20	2

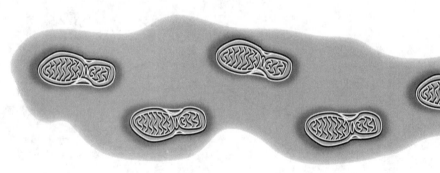

1. $95 \div 9 =$
2. $475 \div 10 =$
3. $590 \div 10 =$
4. $1,000 \div 5 =$
5. $750 \div 375 =$
6. $1,000 \div 25 =$
7. $475 \div 50 =$
8. $95 \div 30 =$
9. $95 \div 15 =$
10. $475 \div 100 =$
11. $750 \div 50 =$
12. $590 \div 50 =$
13. $750 \div 75 =$
14. $475 \div 25 =$
15. $1,000 \div 50 =$
16. $1,000 \div 10 =$

12

NCTM Standard: Number and Operations – compute fluently and make reasonable estimates

Round the dividend (the first number) to the greatest place value and divide, and then find the answer to each problem in the boxes to the right.

CART OFF SOME QUOTIENTS

0.2	15	2.5	0.05
0.8	4	1.6	30
1	10	3	1.25
45	0.09	2	0.08

1. $0.45 \div 10 =$
2. $6.5 \div 7 =$
3. $8.6 \div 3 =$
4. $0.89 \div 10 =$
5. $0.36 \div 5 =$
6. $0.95 \div 5 =$
7. $5.6 \div 3 =$
8. $3.6 \div 5 =$
9. $0.75 \div 0.5 =$
10. $5.7 \div 0.2 =$
11. $7.8 \div 2 =$
12. $9.2 \div 0.2 =$
13. $4.7 \div 2 =$
14. $4.8 \div 4 =$
15. $5.9 \div 0.6 =$
16. $5.8 \div 0.4 =$

13

NCTM Standard: Number and Operations – compute fluently and make reasonable estimates

Grapple for Some Quotients

Round the dividend (the first number) to a compatible number and divide, and then find the answer to each problem in the boxes to the right.

400	220	100	10
110	70	90	40
240	130	20	80
50	7	120	60

1. $542 \div 6 =$
2. $657 \div 8 =$
3. $492 \div 7 =$
4. $428 \div 60 =$
5. $809 \div 2 =$
6. $249 \div 4 =$
7. $328 \div 8 =$
8. $263 \div 2 =$
9. $719 \div 7 =$
10. $558 \div 5 =$
11. $359 \div 3 =$
12. $449 \div 2 =$
13. $298 \div 6 =$
14. $192 \div 9 =$
15. $489 \div 2 =$
16. $218 \div 20 =$

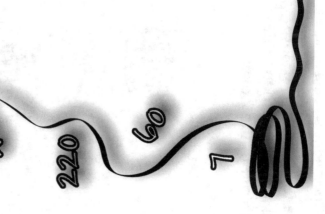

14

NCTM Standard: Number and Operations – understand ways of representing numbers and work flexibly with fractions

CLIP LOWEST COMMON DENOMINATORS

Find the least common denominator for each pair of fractions below, and then find the answer in the boxes to the right.

30	4	45	40
18	9	6	72
56	12	24	35
28	20	15	21

1. $\frac{1}{2}$ and $\frac{1}{4}$

2. $\frac{3}{8}$ and $\frac{4}{9}$

3. $\frac{1}{4}$ and $\frac{5}{6}$

4. $\frac{5}{9}$ and $\frac{5}{6}$

5. $\frac{6}{7}$ and $\frac{2}{3}$

6. $\frac{3}{8}$ and $\frac{4}{5}$

7. $\frac{3}{4}$ and $\frac{3}{7}$

8. $\frac{5}{6}$ and $\frac{3}{8}$

9. $\frac{2}{3}$ and $\frac{2}{9}$

10. $\frac{3}{5}$ and $\frac{1}{4}$

11. $\frac{1}{5}$ and $\frac{2}{3}$

12. $\frac{1}{6}$ and $\frac{1}{3}$

13. $\frac{5}{9}$ and $\frac{2}{5}$

14. $\frac{7}{8}$ and $\frac{6}{7}$

15. $\frac{1}{5}$ and $\frac{2}{7}$

16. $\frac{2}{5}$ and $\frac{5}{6}$

NCTM Standard: Number and Operations – understand ways of representing numbers and work flexibly with fractions

Conquest Over Common Denominators

Reduce each pair of fractions to lowest terms, and then find the matching pair in the boxes to the right.

1. $\frac{4}{20}$ and $\frac{5}{20}$
2. $\frac{4}{10}$ and $\frac{5}{10}$
3. $\frac{1}{4}$ and $\frac{2}{4}$
4. $\frac{15}{20}$ and $\frac{16}{20}$
5. $\frac{15}{20}$ and $\frac{8}{20}$
6. $\frac{5}{10}$ and $\frac{8}{10}$
7. $\frac{9}{12}$ and $\frac{4}{12}$
8. $\frac{3}{12}$ and $\frac{4}{12}$
9. $\frac{3}{12}$ and $\frac{8}{12}$
10. $\frac{1}{6}$ and $\frac{2}{6}$
11. $\frac{2}{6}$ and $\frac{5}{6}$
12. $\frac{4}{6}$ and $\frac{5}{6}$
13. $\frac{12}{15}$ and $\frac{5}{15}$
14. $\frac{6}{15}$ and $\frac{10}{15}$
15. $\frac{16}{20}$ and $\frac{5}{20}$
16. $\frac{3}{15}$ and $\frac{5}{15}$

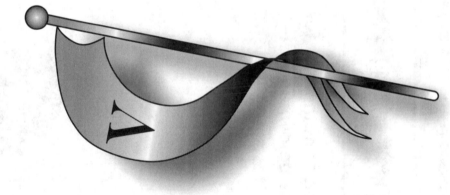

$\frac{1}{4}$ and $\frac{1}{2}$	$\frac{1}{4}$ and $\frac{2}{3}$	$\frac{2}{5}$ and $\frac{1}{2}$	$\frac{3}{4}$ and $\frac{4}{5}$
$\frac{2}{3}$ and $\frac{5}{6}$	$\frac{1}{5}$ and $\frac{1}{4}$	$\frac{1}{5}$ and $\frac{1}{3}$	$\frac{1}{2}$ and $\frac{4}{5}$
$\frac{1}{3}$ and $\frac{5}{6}$	$\frac{3}{4}$ and $\frac{1}{3}$	$\frac{1}{4}$ and $\frac{1}{3}$	$\frac{2}{5}$ and $\frac{2}{3}$
$\frac{3}{4}$ and $\frac{2}{5}$	$\frac{1}{6}$ and $\frac{1}{3}$	$\frac{4}{5}$ and $\frac{1}{3}$	$\frac{4}{5}$ and $\frac{1}{4}$

NCTM Standard: Number and Operations – compute fluently and work flexibly with fractions

Find an Improper Fraction

Match each mixed number below with an improper fraction in the boxes to the right.

1. $3\frac{2}{3}$

2. $3\frac{7}{9}$

3. $1\frac{5}{7}$

4. $7\frac{2}{3}$

5. $2\frac{1}{7}$

6. $1\frac{8}{9}$

7. $4\frac{1}{6}$

8. $3\frac{1}{5}$

9. $15\frac{2}{5}$

10. $8\frac{6}{7}$

11. $13\frac{1}{4}$

12. $1\frac{6}{8}$

13. $1\frac{5}{8}$

14. $4\frac{8}{9}$

15. $3\frac{2}{7}$

16. $7\frac{5}{9}$

$\frac{15}{7}$	$\frac{53}{4}$	$\frac{23}{7}$	$\frac{23}{3}$
$\frac{12}{7}$	$\frac{16}{5}$	$\frac{13}{8}$	$\frac{25}{6}$
$\frac{14}{8}$	$\frac{17}{9}$	$\frac{11}{3}$	$\frac{68}{9}$
$\frac{77}{5}$	$\frac{34}{9}$	$\frac{44}{9}$	$\frac{62}{7}$

NCTM Standard: Number and Operations – understand fractions as part of a collection

Hook Fractions as Part of a Collection

Name each fraction that is represented by the gray shapes below, and then find the answer in lowest terms in the boxes to the right.

$\frac{4}{11}$	$\frac{7}{10}$	$\frac{2}{3}$	$\frac{8}{9}$
$\frac{4}{7}$	$\frac{1}{2}$	$\frac{3}{10}$	$\frac{7}{11}$
$\frac{5}{12}$	$\frac{5}{9}$	$\frac{6}{11}$	$\frac{8}{11}$
$\frac{4}{5}$	$\frac{3}{4}$	$\frac{3}{8}$	$\frac{7}{12}$

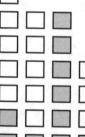

1.
2.
3.
4.
5.
6.
7.
8.
9.
10.
11.
12.
13.
14.
15.
16.

18

NCTM Standard: Number and Operations – understand fractions as part of a collection

Lasso Fractions in a Collection

Name each fraction that is represented by the black dots below, reduce the fraction to lowest terms, and then find the answer in the boxes to the right.

$\frac{3}{7}$	$\frac{5}{13}$	$\frac{6}{17}$	$\frac{4}{11}$
$\frac{2}{3}$	$\frac{9}{14}$	$\frac{6}{13}$	$\frac{1}{3}$
$\frac{6}{7}$	$\frac{1}{2}$	$\frac{1}{6}$	$\frac{2}{5}$
$\frac{4}{5}$	$\frac{1}{5}$	$\frac{3}{5}$	$\frac{1}{4}$

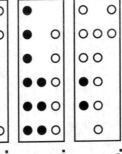
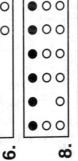
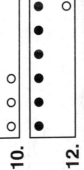
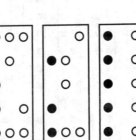

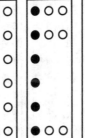
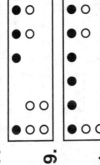
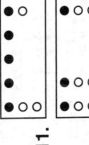
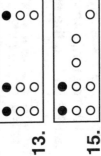

1.
2.
3.
4.
5.
6.
7.
8.
9.
10.
11.
12.
13.
14.
15.
16.

19

NCTM Standard: Number and Operations – understand ways of representing numbers and work flexibly with fractions

Using the black dots as the numerator and the gray dots as the denominator, reduce the fraction to lowest terms, and then find the answer in the boxes to the right.

Reduce Those Fractions!

$1\frac{1}{8}$	$\frac{8}{9}$	$\frac{4}{7}$	$\frac{1}{5}$
$1\frac{1}{2}$	$1\frac{2}{3}$	$1\frac{1}{4}$	$\frac{3}{5}$
$\frac{4}{9}$	$\frac{1}{3}$	$\frac{1}{4}$	$\frac{2}{5}$
$\frac{7}{9}$	$\frac{4}{5}$	$\frac{5}{6}$	$1\frac{1}{5}$

1.
2.
3.
4.
5.
6.
7.
8.
9.
10.
11.
12.
13.
14.
15.
16.

20

NCTM Standard: Number and Operations – understand ways of representing numbers

Snatch the Least Common Multiple

Find the least common multiple of each of the following pairs of numbers in the boxes to the right.

1. 8 and 4
2. 9 and 4
3. 8 and 5
4. 9 and 10
5. 6 and 4
6. 6 and 3
7. 8 and 16
8. 8 and 9
9. 9 and 6
10. 4 and 7
11. 5 and 10
12. 5 and 3
13. 15 and 10
14. 14 and 21
15. 12 and 20

36	12	42
60	40	30
16	10	8
72	90	28
15	6	18

NCTM Standard: Number and Operations – understand fractions as part of a collection and on a number line

Secure Some Fractions

Determine the fraction that would be at the arrow on each number line below, and then find that fraction in the boxes to the right.

$2\frac{3}{8}$	$3\frac{1}{4}$	6	$3\frac{3}{8}$
$2\frac{2}{16}$	$7\frac{3}{4}$	$2\frac{1}{8}$	5
$1\frac{1}{4}$	$5\frac{7}{8}$	$1\frac{5}{8}$	$4\frac{3}{4}$
$5\frac{2}{8}$	$4\frac{5}{8}$	$2\frac{3}{4}$	$1\frac{2}{8}$

1.   5 — 7
2.   7 — 8
3.   1 — $1\frac{1}{2}$
4. $2\frac{1}{2}$ — 3
5.   4 — 6
6. $1\frac{1}{2}$ — $1\frac{3}{4}$
7. $2\frac{1}{4}$ — $2\frac{1}{2}$
8. $1\frac{1}{8}$ — $1\frac{3}{8}$
9. $2\frac{1}{16}$ — $2\frac{3}{16}$
10. $3\frac{1}{4}$ — $3\frac{4}{8}$
11. $4\frac{1}{2}$ — 5
12.   2 — $2\frac{1}{4}$
13.   3 — $3\frac{1}{2}$
14.   4 — 5
15. $5\frac{1}{2}$ — 6
16. $5\frac{1}{8}$ — $5\frac{3}{8}$

NCTM Standard: Number and Operations – understand fractions as part of a collection and on a number line

Snap Up Fractions on a Number Line

Determine the fraction that would be at the arrow on each number line below, and then find that fraction in the boxes to the right.

7	$17\frac{1}{2}$	$2\frac{1}{16}$
$4\frac{3}{4}$	$1\frac{1}{4}$	5
$3\frac{1}{2}$	$5\frac{1}{8}$	$1\frac{3}{4}$
$3\frac{3}{4}$	4	$1\frac{1}{16}$
$1\frac{3}{8}$	$1\frac{1}{8}$	$5\frac{7}{8}$

1. 17 ——————— 18
2. 1 ——————— 2
3. 3 ——————— 4
4. 1 ——————— 2
5. 3 ——————— 5
6. 6 ——————— 9
7. 3 ——————— 7
8. 3 ——————— 4
9. 1 ——————— 2
10. 1 ——————— $1\frac{1}{2}$
11. 1 ——————— $1\frac{1}{4}$
12. 2 ——————— $2\frac{1}{2}$
13. 4 ——————— 5
14. 5 ——————— 6
15. 5 ——————— 6

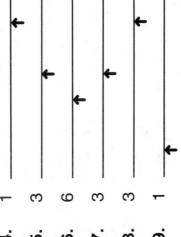
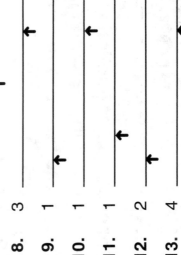

23

NCTM Standard: Number and Operations – understand ways of representing numbers and work flexibly with fractions

STAMP OUT COMMON DENOMINATORS

For each pair of fractions below, find the fractions with the common denominators in the boxes to the right.

1. $\frac{6}{7}$ and $\frac{2}{3}$
2. $\frac{1}{4}$ and $\frac{5}{6}$
3. $\frac{1}{2}$ and $\frac{1}{4}$
4. $\frac{2}{3}$ and $\frac{2}{9}$
5. $\frac{3}{4}$ and $\frac{3}{7}$
6. $\frac{1}{6}$ and $\frac{1}{3}$
7. $\frac{7}{8}$ and $\frac{6}{7}$
8. $\frac{1}{5}$ and $\frac{2}{3}$
9. $\frac{3}{5}$ and $\frac{1}{4}$
10. $\frac{1}{3}$ and $\frac{2}{9}$
11. $\frac{5}{9}$ and $\frac{2}{5}$
12. $\frac{5}{6}$ and $\frac{3}{8}$
13. $\frac{3}{8}$ and $\frac{4}{5}$
14. $\frac{5}{9}$ and $\frac{5}{6}$
15. $\frac{3}{8}$ and $\frac{2}{9}$

$\frac{1}{6}$ and $\frac{2}{6}$	$\frac{20}{24}$ and $\frac{9}{24}$	$\frac{3}{15}$ and $\frac{10}{15}$
$\frac{10}{18}$ and $\frac{15}{18}$	$\frac{49}{56}$ and $\frac{48}{56}$	$\frac{3}{12}$ and $\frac{10}{12}$
$\frac{3}{9}$ and $\frac{2}{9}$	$\frac{18}{21}$ and $\frac{14}{21}$	$\frac{6}{9}$ and $\frac{2}{9}$
$\frac{27}{72}$ and $\frac{16}{72}$	$\frac{21}{28}$ and $\frac{12}{28}$	$\frac{15}{40}$ and $\frac{32}{40}$
$\frac{12}{20}$ and $\frac{5}{20}$	$\frac{25}{45}$ and $\frac{18}{45}$	$\frac{2}{4}$ and $\frac{1}{4}$

NCTM Standard: Number and Operations – compute fluently

Triumph Over Adding Fractions

Solve each problem below, reduce to lowest terms, and then find the answer in the boxes to the right.

$\frac{3}{4}$	$1\frac{3}{10}$	$\frac{4}{9}$	$\frac{7}{10}$
$1\frac{1}{5}$	$1\frac{1}{3}$	1	$1\frac{2}{5}$
$1\frac{3}{5}$	$\frac{7}{8}$	$\frac{1}{2}$	$\frac{2}{3}$
$1\frac{1}{2}$	$1\frac{1}{6}$	$1\frac{1}{7}$	$\frac{11}{15}$

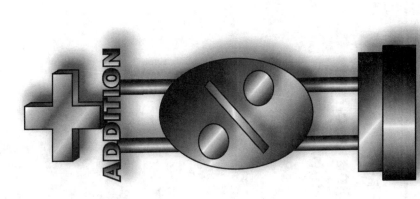

1. $\frac{1}{2} + \frac{1}{2} =$

2. $\frac{1}{4} + \frac{2}{4} =$

3. $\frac{4}{5} + \frac{3}{5} =$

4. $\frac{2}{8} + \frac{5}{8} =$

5. $\frac{1}{3} + \frac{1}{3} =$

6. $\frac{3}{10} + \frac{4}{10} =$

7. $\frac{1}{6} + \frac{2}{6} =$

8. $\frac{7}{10} + \frac{9}{10} =$

9. $\frac{3}{4} + \frac{3}{4} =$

10. $\frac{6}{10} + \frac{7}{10} =$

11. $\frac{5}{6} + \frac{3}{6} =$

12. $\frac{5}{7} + \frac{3}{7} =$

13. $\frac{5}{12} + \frac{9}{12} =$

14. $\frac{4}{15} + \frac{7}{15} =$

15. $\frac{6}{15} + \frac{12}{15} =$

16. $\frac{5}{18} + \frac{3}{18} =$

NCTM Standard: Number and Operations – understand ways of representing numbers and work flexibly with fractions, decimals, and percents

Button Down Fractions and Decimals

For each of the fractions below, find the corresponding decimal in the boxes to the right.

1. $1\frac{1}{2}$
2. $3\frac{1}{4}$
3. $3\frac{1}{8}$
4. $5\frac{2}{8}$
5. $1\frac{1}{4}$
6. $\frac{1}{2}$
7. $\frac{1}{5}$
8. $1\frac{1}{5}$
9. $3\frac{1}{2}$
10. $5\frac{1}{5}$
11. $6\frac{1}{5}$
12. $1\frac{1}{8}$
13. $3\frac{3}{8}$
14. $1\frac{2}{5}$
15. $3\frac{5}{8}$

6.2	0.2	3.5
5.25	1.2	3.25
1.25	1.5	1.125
3.625	5.2	0.5
3.375	3.125	1.4

26

NCTM Standard: Number and Operations – understand ways of representing numbers and work flexibly with fractions, decimals, and percents

Collar Some Multiples

4	30	16	15
60	2	10	5
75	70	50	2.5
100	45	20	25

Mentally calculate each problem below, and then find the answer in the boxes to the right.

1. 25% of 400 =

2. $\frac{1}{2}$ of 40 =

3. 0.1 of 20 =

4. 50% of 30 =

5. 75% of 80 =

6. $\frac{1}{3}$ of 90 =

7. 0.5 of 50 =

8. 50% of 150 =

9. 25% of 20 =

10. $\frac{1}{4}$ of 200 =

11. $\frac{1}{5}$ of 50 =

12. $\frac{1}{3}$ of 210 =

13. 0.4 of 10 =

14. 0.25 of 10 =

15. 0.5 of 90 =

16. 20% of 80 =

27

NCTM Standard: Number and Operations – understand ways of representing numbers and work flexibly with fractions, decimals, and percents

Salvage Lots of Percent Equivalents

225%	75%	37.5%	275%
12.5%	30%	20%	25%
60%	50%	87.5%	150%
40%	125%	80%	62.5%

For each fraction below, find the corresponding percentage in the boxes to the right.

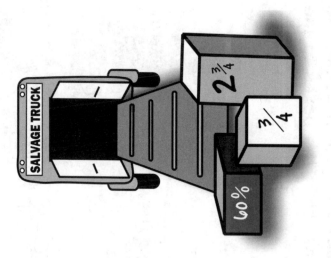

1. $\frac{1}{2}$
2. $\frac{1}{4}$
3. $\frac{1}{5}$
4. $\frac{2}{5}$
5. $\frac{4}{5}$
6. $\frac{3}{4}$
7. $\frac{1}{8}$
8. $1\frac{1}{2}$
9. $2\frac{1}{4}$
10. $1\frac{1}{4}$
11. $2\frac{3}{4}$
12. $\frac{3}{5}$
13. $\frac{3}{8}$
14. $\frac{5}{8}$
15. $\frac{7}{8}$
16. $\frac{3}{10}$

NCTM Standard: Number and Operations – compute fluently and make reasonable estimates

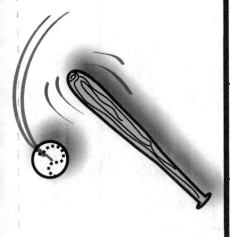

Strike Out Some Mixed Numbers

For each decimal below, find the corresponding fraction in lowest terms in the boxes to the right.

1. 5.25
2. 3.5
3. 1.55
4. 3.75
5. 5.5
6. 3.25
7. 5.125
8. 5.375
9. 7.05
10. 5.05
11. 7.125
12. 3.375
13. 2.25

14. 7.5
15. 5.625
16. 2.75
17. 5.75
18. 7.25
19. 2.5
20. 5.1
21. 7.2
22. 5.2
23. 2.6
24. 7.8
25. 3.9

$5\frac{3}{8}$	$5\frac{1}{20}$	$2\frac{3}{5}$	$3\frac{3}{4}$	$2\frac{1}{4}$
$7\frac{4}{5}$	$5\frac{1}{4}$	$5\frac{3}{4}$	$7\frac{1}{20}$	$5\frac{1}{10}$
$5\frac{1}{2}$	$7\frac{1}{4}$	$3\frac{1}{2}$	$7\frac{1}{5}$	$7\frac{1}{2}$
$3\frac{3}{8}$	$2\frac{1}{2}$	$1\frac{11}{20}$	$2\frac{3}{4}$	$5\frac{1}{8}$
$3\frac{9}{10}$	$3\frac{1}{4}$	$5\frac{1}{5}$	$7\frac{1}{8}$	$5\frac{5}{8}$

29

NCTM Standard: Number and Operations – compute fluently; work flexibly with percents to solve problems or estimate answers

Pounce on a Percent

Find the answer to each problem below in the boxes to the right.

1. 2% of 100 =
2. 25% of 12 =
3. 50% of 20 =
4. 50% of 80 =
5. 50% of 100 =
6. 25% of 120 =
7. 25% of 4 =
8. 25% of 36 =
9. 75% of 28 =
10. 75% of 16 =
11. 75% of 20 =
12. 20% of 100 =
13. 20% of 40 =
14. 20% of 70 =
15. 25% of 20 =
16. 5% of 80 =

1	20	15	40
3	4	2	14
21	10	5	9
12	30	8	50

NCTM Standard: Number and Operations – understand ways of representing numbers and work flexibly with percents

Find what percent the black dots are in relation to the gray dots for each of the problems below, and then find the answer in the boxes to the right.

Round Up Percents

90%	100%	120%
50%	10%	70%
140%	20%	80%
130%	150%	110%
30%	60%	40%

150% 80% 40% 110% 90%

1.
2.
3.
4.
5.
6.
7.
8.
9.
10.
11.
12.
13.
14.
15.

NCTM Standard: Number and Operations – understand the place-value structure of the base ten system

Read the words below, and then find the numbers represented by the words in the boxes to the right.

1. four hundred thousand, two

2. four hundred twenty thousand, two

3. four hundred two thousand, two hundred two

4. eight hundred eighteen thousand, three hundred twenty

5. eight hundred thousand, four

6. four hundred twenty thousand, forty

7. eight hundred twelve thousand, thirty-two

8. four hundred three thousand, twenty

9. eight hundred three thousand, fifty-two

10. four hundred forty-four thousand, two

11. eight hundred twenty-three thousand, forty-five

12. forty thousand, twenty

13. eighty thousand, twenty

14. eighty-three thousand, twenty

15. eighty-three thousand, two

Bag Some Huge Numbers

400,002	40,020	818,320
444,002	402,202	83,002
800,004	83,020	420,040
823,045	420,002	80,020
812,032	803,052	403,020

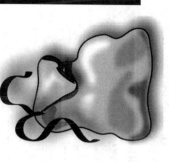

NCTM Standard: Number and Operations – understand the place-value structure of the base ten system

Read the words below, and then find the numbers represented by the words in the boxes to the right.

1. four hundred twenty thousand, five hundred two
2. three hundred fifteen thousand, two hundred six
3. fifteen thousand, four hundred twenty-four
4. thirty-seven thousand, two hundred forty-nine
5. three hundred seventy-five thousand, six hundred two
6. eight hundred thousand, sixty-seven
7. ten thousand, five hundred six
8. seventeen thousand, four hundred two
9. seven hundred five thousand, five hundred five
10. sixty-four thousand, two hundred forty
11. seventy-five thousand, six hundred four
12. thirty thousand, two hundred fifty-one
13. six hundred forty thousand, seven
14. two hundred thousand, six
15. three hundred two thousand, seven
16. seven hundred three thousand, two hundred three

Bring in Some Big Numbers

17,402	640,007	315,206	75,604
800,067	703,203	705,505	15,424
200,006	420,502	10,506	37,249
30,251	375,602	302,007	64,240

NCTM Standard: Number and Operations – understand the place-value structure of the base ten system

Grab Base Ten Number Representations

Determine the number represented in expanded form below, and then find the answer in the boxes to the right.

572	542	551	249
232	253	537	555
229	265	543	583
228	261	532	238

1. 3 ones, 2 hundreds, 5 tens
2. 2 hundreds, 3 tens, 2 ones
3. 4 tens, 3 ones, 5 hundreds
4. 2 ones, 5 hundreds, 4 tens
5. 8 ones, 2 hundreds, 3 tens
6. 4 tens, 9 ones, 2 hundreds
7. 5 tens, 5 ones, 5 hundreds
8. 2 tens, 2 hundreds, 8 ones
9. 1 one, 6 tens, 2 hundreds
10. 6 tens, 2 hundreds, 5 ones
11. 7 tens, 5 hundreds, 2 ones
12. 7 ones, 3 tens, 5 hundreds
13. 1 one, 5 hundreds, 5 tens
14. 3 tens, 5 hundreds, 2 ones
15. 8 tens, 3 ones, 5 hundreds
16. 9 ones, 2 tens, 2 hundreds

NCTM Standard: Number and Operations – understand the place-value structure of the base ten system

Determine the place value of the underlined digits below, and find the answer in the boxes to the right.

Pull in Some Place Value

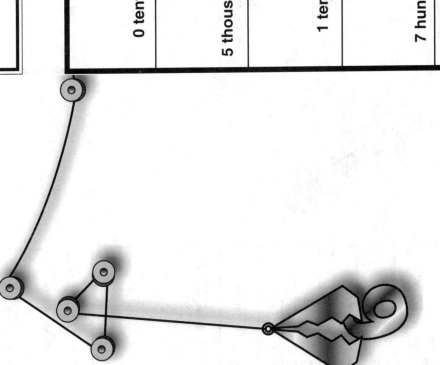

0 tenths	4 hundredths	6 thousandths
5 thousandths	9 ten thousandths	8 tens
1 tenth	8 thousandths	8 hundred thousandths
7 hundreds	1 hundred thousandth	0 hundredths
5 tenths	8 ones	6 tenths

1. 1.34<u>5</u>8
2. 5.268<u>9</u>
3. 63.2900<u>1</u>
4. 102.<u>5</u>76
5. 7<u>8</u>.2509
6. 2.2000<u>8</u>
7. 5.<u>1</u>0987
8. 61.34<u>5</u>
9. <u>8</u>1.3450
10. 0.79<u>8</u>63
11. 7.6<u>5</u>931
12. <u>7</u>07.12
13. 4.20<u>9</u>86
14. 51.<u>0</u>981
15. 786.34<u>6</u>901

NCTM Standard: Number and Operations – understand and use ratios to represent quantitative relationships

Determine the ratio of black dots to gray dots for each of the problems below, and then find the answer in lowest terms in the boxes to the right.

DRAW IN RATIOS

$\frac{7}{9}$	$5\frac{2}{3}$	$1\frac{3}{11}$
$\frac{5}{9}$	$\frac{1}{4}$	$1\frac{4}{11}$
$2\frac{1}{8}$	1	$\frac{3}{4}$
$1\frac{1}{4}$	$\frac{12}{17}$	$1\frac{4}{9}$
$\frac{10}{11}$	2	$3\frac{2}{5}$

1.
2.
3.
4.
5.
6.
7.
8.
9.
10.
11.
12.
13.
14.
15.

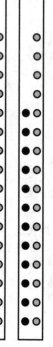
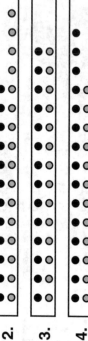
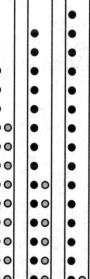
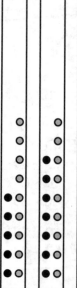
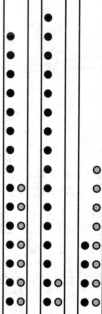
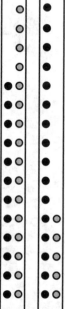
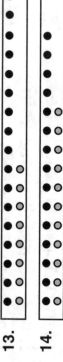
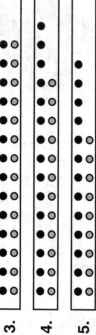

36

NCTM Standard: Number and Operations – understand ways of representing numbers and work flexibly with ratios

Rack Up Ratios

5:12	5:2	3:1
5:3	7:11	13:8
1:1	4:15	3:2
2:3	7:4	3:5
4:5	15:13	2:1

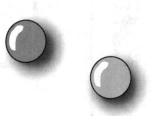

Determine the ratio of black dots to gray dots, and then find the ratio in lowest terms in the boxes to the right.

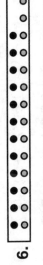
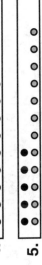
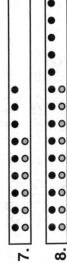

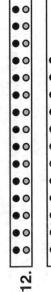
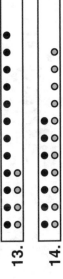

1.
2.
3.
4.
5.
6.
7.
8.
9.
10.
11.
12.
13.
14.
15.

NCTM Standard: Number and Operations – compute fluently and make reasonable estimates

Drag in Addition Estimation Answers

Round the numbers in each problem below to the largest place value, add, and then find the answer in the boxes to the right.

15,000	9,000	6,000
13,000	18,000	8,000
16,000	12,000	10,000
5,000	11,000	4,000
14,000	19,000	7,000

1. 3,458 + 9,432 =
2. 4,562 + 7,811 =
3. 5,678 + 2,132 =
4. 2,315 + 2,564 =
5. 5,672 + 1,256 =
6. 7,501 + 2,341 =
7. 4,579 + 3,910 =
8. 2,199 + 2,446 =
9. 4,256 + 7,199 =
10. 6,100 + 8,256 =
11. 5,298 + 1,459 =
12. 7,890 + 8,154 =
13. 7,190 + 8,499 =
14. 9,199 + 9,988 =
15. 8,900 + 9,199 =

NCTM Standard: Number and Operations – compute fluently and make reasonable estimates

ROPE SOME AVERAGES

Round each number below to the largest place value, and then find their sum's approximate average in the boxes to the right.

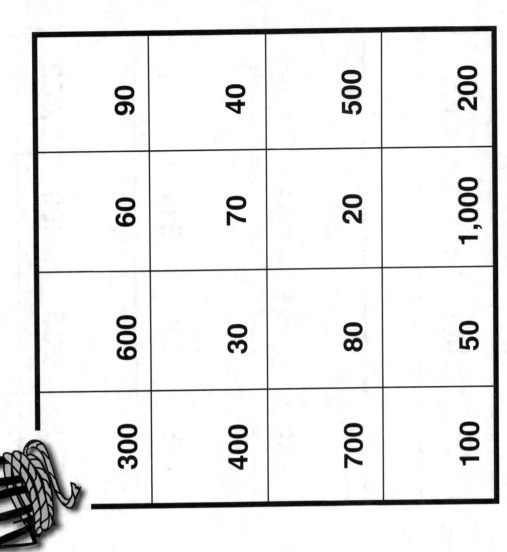

300	600	60	90
400	30	70	40
700	80	20	500
100	50	1,000	200

1. 13 + 42 + 36 =

2. 56 + 22 + 97 =

3. 21 + 24 + 23 =

4. 728 + 678 + 690 + 710 =

5. 202 + 200 + 202 =

6. 260 + 250 + 325 =

7. 540 + 510 + 210 =

8. 25 + 34 + 69 + 29 =

9. 39 + 79 + 58 + 21 =

10. 97 + 98 + 99 + 95 =

11. 45 + 68 + 91 + 71 =

12. 95 + 81 + 92 + 91 =

13. 79 + 82 + 81 + 78 =

14. 510 + 529 + 498 + 476 =

15. 985 + 1,463 + 990 =

16. 590 + 649 + 629 + 597 =

NCTM Standard: Number and Operations – compute fluently and make reasonable estimates

Using mental math only, choose the answer for each subtraction problem from the boxes to the right.

Peg Subtraction Answers

159	2,121	296	1,457
775	36	317	811
851	235	390	2,062
511	591	642	850

1. 394 - 235 =
2. 756 - 521 =
3. 984 - 342 =
4. 1,238 - 921 =
5. 2,721 - 659 =
6. 742 - 231 =
7. 896 - 121 =
8. 2,548 - 1,091 =
9. 2,245 - 124 =
10. 521 - 131 =
11. 982 - 131 =
12. 942 - 131 =
13. 134 - 98 =
14. 385 - 89 =
15. 879 - 29 =
16. 780 - 189 =

40

NCTM Standard: Number and Operations – identify and use relationships between operations, such as the commutative property

BUTTON DOWN THE COMMUTATIVE PROPERTY

For each problem below, find the corresponding problem that shows the commutative property in the boxes to the right.

22 x 15 x 16 =	16 + 13 + 17 =	31 x 15 x 22 =
20 + 23 + 22 =	20 x 21 x 22 =	27 + 20 + 21 =
22 + 27 + 25 =	12 + 13 + 15 =	26 + 25 + 20 =
12 + 16 + 20 =	20 + 27 + 22 =	25 x 15 x 23 =
25 x 22 x 30 =	16 + 14 + 20 =	26 x 20 x 25 =

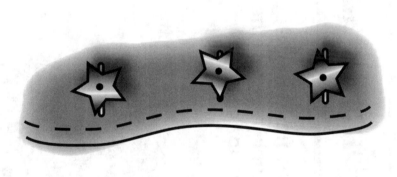

1. 14 + 16 + 20 =
2. 22 x 16 x 15 =
3. 13 + 17 + 16 =
4. 23 x 25 x 15 =
5. 20 x 22 x 21 =
6. 20 + 25 + 26 =
7. 20 + 22 + 27 =
8. 23 + 22 + 20 =
9. 25 + 22 + 27 =
10. 15 x 22 x 31 =
11. 13 + 12 + 15 =
12. 25 x 26 x 20 =
13. 20 + 21 + 27 =
14. 16 + 20 + 12 =
15. 30 x 25 x 22 =

NCTM Standard: Number and Operations – compute fluently and make reasonable estimates

Latch Onto Square Root Estimations

For each number below, find the exact square root or a reasonable range of the square root in the boxes to the right.

25	between 12 and 13	between 5 and 6
between 3 and 4	between 1 and 2	between 14 and 15
between 8 and 9	between 15 and 16	between 7 and 8
between 13 and 14	between 4 and 5	20
between 11 and 12	30	between 9 and 10

1. 26
2. 250
3. 17
4. 68
5. 85
6. 150
7. 50
8. 10
9. 3
10. 125
11. 180
12. 200
13. 400
14. 625
15. 900

NCTM Standard: Number and Operations – understand ways of representing numbers, use exponential notation

OVERCOME EXPONENTS

125	4	16	121
100	8	27	25
64	256	36	32
49	9	144	81

Find the values of the numbers with exponents below in the boxes to the right.

1. 2^2

2. 3^2

3. 4^2

4. 5^2

5. 6^2

6. 10^2

7. 8^2

8. 7^2

9. 9^2

10. 3^3

11. 4^4

12. 11^2

13. 2^3

14. 5^3

15. 12^2

16. 2^5

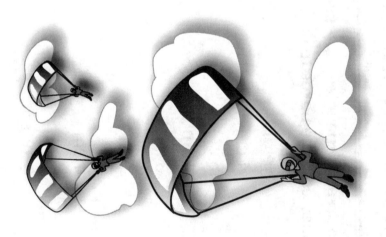

NCTM Standard: Geometry – analyze properties of two-dimensional shapes; **Measurement** – apply appropriate formulas to determine measurements

CRUNCH THE AREA OF TRIANGLES

Calculate each of the areas of triangles represented below and find the answer in the boxes to the right.

Length of Base	Height
1. 12 cm	4 cm
2. 5 in.	6 in.
3. 4 cm	4 cm
4. 4 in.	8 in.
5. 5 cm	4 cm
6. 9 in.	4 in.
7. 10 cm	4 cm
8. 12 in.	5 in.
9. 7 in.	6 in.
10. 9 in.	6 in.
11. 8 cm	8 cm
12. 5 in.	5 in.
13. 6 in.	2 in.
14. 7 in.	4 in.
15. 10 cm	5 cm
16. 11 in.	4 in.

16 sq. in.	22 sq. in.	18 sq. in.	32 sq. cm
30 sq. in.	24 sq. cm	25 sq. cm	15 sq. in.
6 sq. in.	12.5 sq. in.	8 sq. cm	27 sq. in.
21 sq. in.	10 sq. cm	14 sq. in.	20 sq. cm

NCTM Standard: Geometry – identify geometric figures

Conquer Geometric Shapes

Match the name of each figure below with its corresponding geometric shape in the boxes to the right.

1. parallelogram
2. square pyramid
3. rhombus
4. trapezoid
5. circle
6. rectangular prism
7. triangular pyramid
8. rectangle
9. triangle
10. hexagonal prism
11. hexagonal pyramid
12. cube
13. square
14. triangular prism
15. cylinder

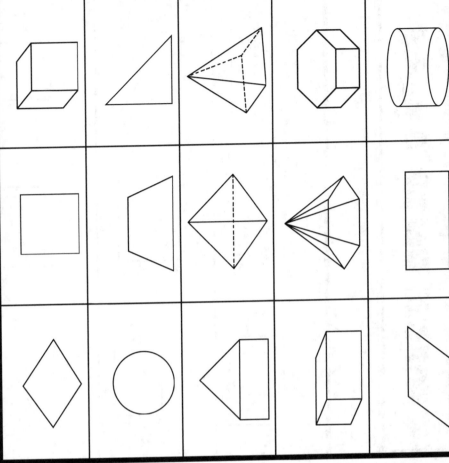

NCTM Standard: Geometry – identify, classify, and understand relationships among two-dimensional objects; understand relations between angles, side lengths, perimeters, and areas; apply the correct formula to solve a problem

LATCH ONTO AREAS

Match each area below with the corresponding geometric shape having that area in the boxes to the right.

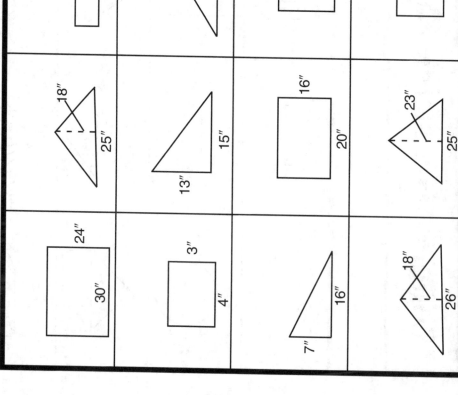

1. 144 square inches

2. 12 square inches

3. 15 square inches

4. 97.5 square inches

5. 287.5 square inches

6. 225 square inches

7. 320 square inches

8. 720 square inches

9. 75 square inches

10. 56 square inches

11. 14 square inches

12. 234 square inches

NCTM Standard: Geometry – specify locations using coordinate geometry

Match the number of the dot on the graph with the coordinates in the boxes to the right.

Master Coordinates

(1,8)	(-8,-2)	(1,-2)	(-3,1)
(6,-4)	(-5,4)	(2,5)	(-2,-2)
(-8,6)	(4,-3)	(-3,9)	(-4,-4)
(-4,5)	(4,5)	(7,10)	(-6,-7)
(8,8)	(4,1)	(8,3)	(7,-7)

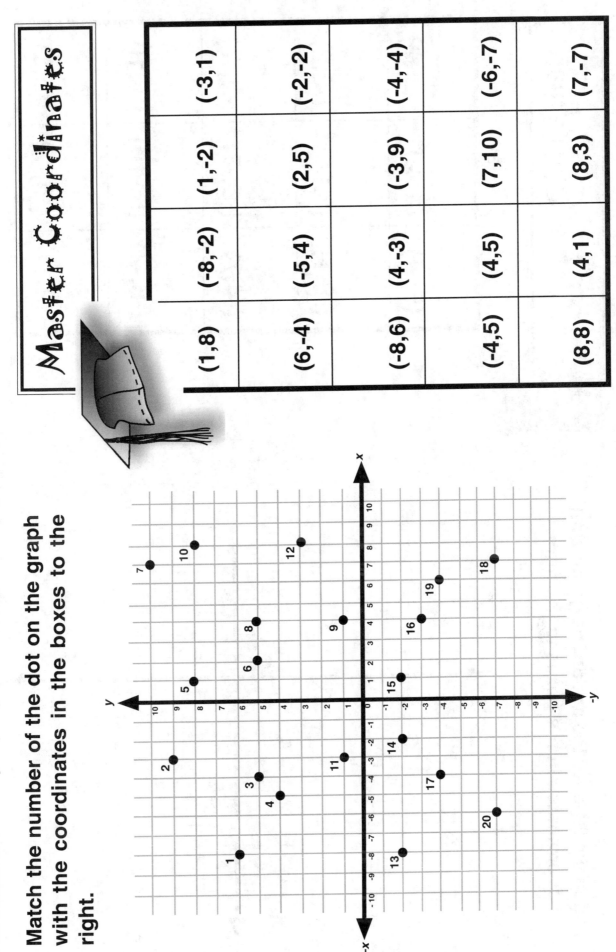

NCTM Standard: Geometry – specify locations using coordinate geometry

Nab a Coordinate

Match the letter of the dot on the graph with the coordinates in the boxes to the right.

(5,-4)	(2,-2)	(-8,-2)
(-8,1)	(8,10)	(-3,2)
(-4,7)	(-5,-8)	(-2,-7)
(-6,-2)	(5,-10)	(-8,10)
(2,1)	(-5,-7)	(5,5)

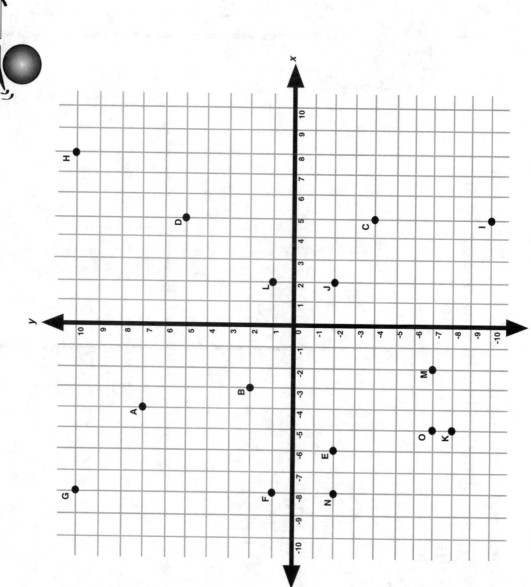

48

NCTM Standard: Geometry – describe, classify, and understand relationships among two-dimensional objects; understand relations between angles, side lengths, perimeters, and areas; apply the correct formula to solve a problem

Play With Perimeters

Match each perimeter below with the corresponding geometric shape having that perimeter in the boxes to the right.

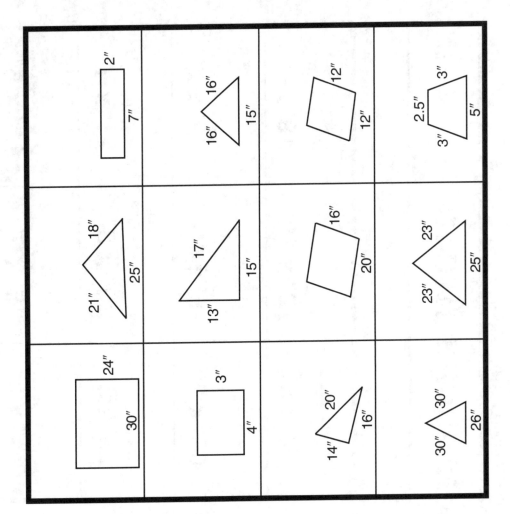

1. 45 inches

2. 13.5 inches

3. 14 inches

4. 18 inches

5. 86 inches

6. 50 inches

7. 47 inches

8. 64 inches

9. 71 inches

10. 108 inches

11. 72 inches

12. 48 inches

NCTM Standard: Geometry – describe, classify, and understand relationships among two-dimensional objects; understand relations between angles, side lengths, perimeters, and areas; apply the correct formula to solve a problem

Reach for Rectangular Areas

Match each area below with the corresponding dimensions in the boxes to the right.

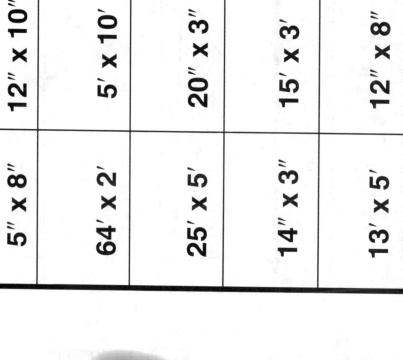

5" x 8'	12" x 10"	18' x 2'
64' x 2'	5' x 10'	52' x 2'
25' x 5'	20" x 3"	21' x 4'
14" x 3"	15' x 3'	11" x 8"
13' x 5'	12" x 8"	16' x 10'

1. 160 ft.²
2. 50 ft.²
3. 60 in.²
4. 40 in.²
5. 36 ft.²
6. 45 ft.²
7. 128 ft.²
8. 120 in.²
9. 42 in.²
10. 125 ft.²
11. 84 ft.²
12. 65 ft.²
13. 96 in.²
14. 88 in.²
15. 104 ft.²

50

NCTM Standard: Algebra – understand patterns; **Geometry** – apply transformations

Snatch Geometric Patterns

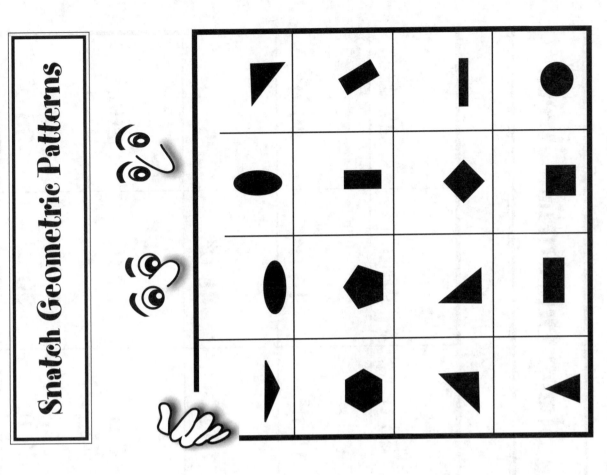

Complete each geometric pattern below with the correct shape in the boxes to the right.

51

NCTM Standard: Geometry – understand relations between angles, side lengths, perimeters, surface areas, and volumes

Stamp Out Surface Areas

Find the surface areas of the shapes below in the boxes to the right. Each square that you see equals one square unit.

34 u²	48 u²	22 u²
18 u²	14 u²	40 u²
10 u²	46 u²	56 u²
6 u²	72 u²	26 u²
42 u²	30 u²	38 u²

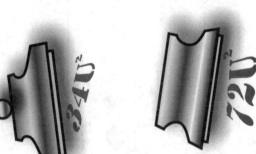

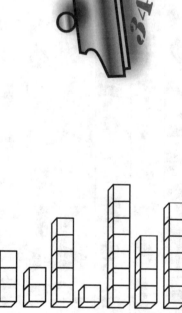

1.
2.
3.
4.
5.
6.
7.
8.
9.
10.
11.
12.
13.
14.
15.

NCTM Standard: Measurement – understand both metric and customary systems of measurement

Crunch Customary Units

Use the inch ruler directly below to measure each of the long boxes beneath it, and then find the answer in the boxes to the right.

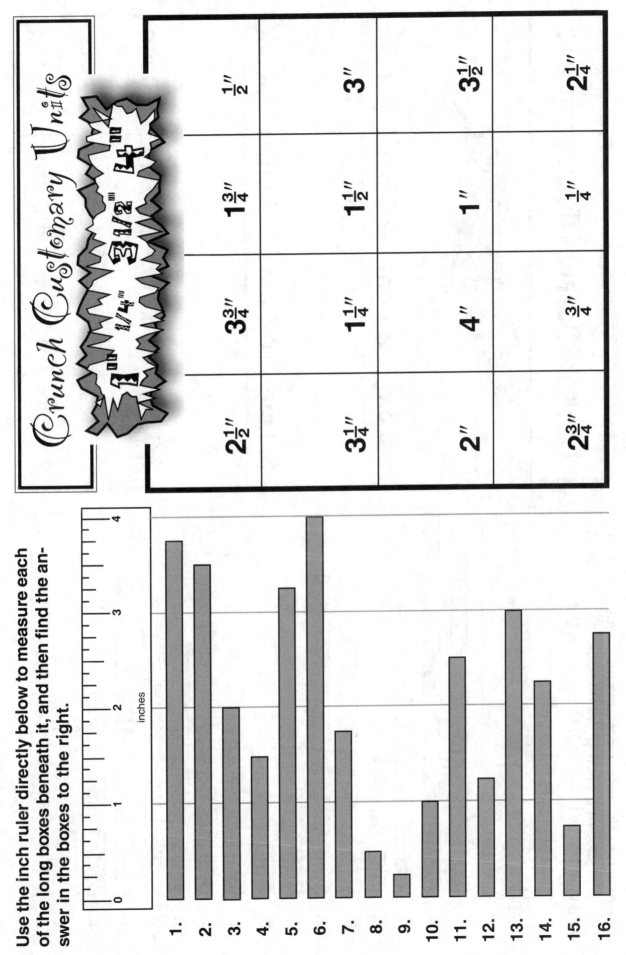

$2\frac{1}{2}''$	$3\frac{3}{4}''$	$1\frac{3}{4}''$	$\frac{1}{2}''$
$3\frac{1}{4}''$	$1\frac{1}{4}''$	$1\frac{1}{2}''$	$3''$
$2''$	$4''$	$1''$	$3\frac{1}{2}''$
$2\frac{3}{4}''$	$\frac{3}{4}''$	$\frac{1}{4}''$	$2\frac{1}{4}''$

53

NCTM Standard: Measurement– understand both metric and customary systems of measurement

The ruler directly below *represents* metric measurement. Use it to measure each of the long boxes beneath it, and then find the answer in the boxes to the right.

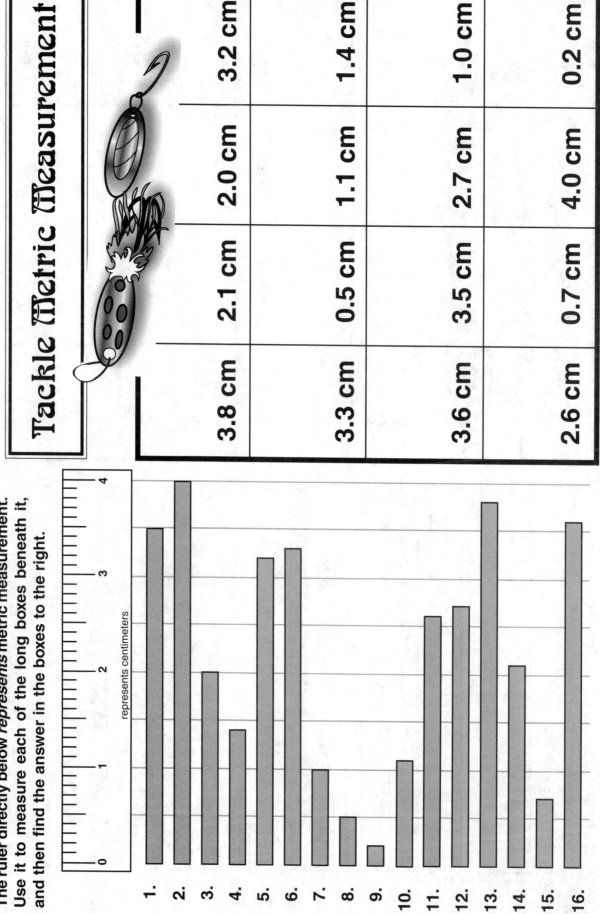

Tackle Metric Measurement

3.8 cm	2.1 cm	2.0 cm	3.2 cm
3.3 cm	0.5 cm	1.1 cm	1.4 cm
3.6 cm	3.5 cm	2.7 cm	1.0 cm
2.6 cm	0.7 cm	4.0 cm	0.2 cm

54

NCTM Standard: Number and Operations – identify and use relationships between operations, such as division as the inverse of multiplication

Grasp the Inverse Operation

For each of the problems below, find the corresponding inverse operation in the boxes to the right.

1. 24 x 6 =
2. 56 x 3 =
3. 33 x 3 =
4. 42 x 3 =
5. 12 x 6 =
6. 15 x 5 =
7. 25 x 5 =
8. 62 x 2 =
9. 52 x 3 =
10. 72 x 3 =
11. 81 x 2 =
12. 92 x 2 =
13. 21 x 6 =
14. 23 x 2 =
15. 52 x 4 =
16. 62 x 3 =

162 ÷ 2 =	124 ÷ 2 =	168 ÷ 3 =	72 ÷ 6 =
126 ÷ 6 =	126 ÷ 3 =	208 ÷ 4 =	144 ÷ 6 =
184 ÷ 2 =	156 ÷ 3 =	125 ÷ 5 =	216 ÷ 3 =
99 ÷ 3 =	46 ÷ 2 =	75 ÷ 5 =	186 ÷ 3 =

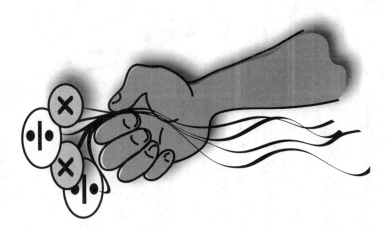

NCTM Standard: Number and Operations – identify and use relationships between operations, such as multiplication as the inverse of division

HAUL IN SOME INVERSE OPERATIONS

90 x 9 =	7 x 30 =	50 x 5 =	70 x 6 =
40 x 6 =	80 x 7 =	90 x 8 =	6 x 50 =
3 x 90 =	70 x 4 =	90 x 7 =	5 x 90 =
9 x 60 =	50 x 7 =	4 x 90 =	8 x 60 =

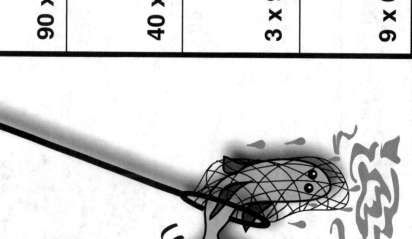

For each of the problems below, find the corresponding inverse operation in the boxes to the right.

1. 560 ÷ 7 =
2. 250 ÷ 5 =
3. 240 ÷ 6 =
4. 280 ÷ 4 =
5. 630 ÷ 7 =
6. 720 ÷ 8 =
7. 810 ÷ 9 =
8. 300 ÷ 6 =
9. 420 ÷ 6 =
10. 480 ÷ 8 =
11. 540 ÷ 9 =
12. 210 ÷ 7 =
13. 270 ÷ 3 =
14. 350 ÷ 7 =
15. 360 ÷ 4 =
16. 450 ÷ 5 =

NCTM Standard: Number and Operations – compute fluently

Round each factor to the nearest ten and then multiply. Find the answer in the boxes to the right.

Snag a Big Multiple

1,800	1,600	2,700	1,500
1,200	1,000	800	3,200
6,300	3,500	2,500	4,900
2,100	3,000	4,800	400

1. 23 × 35 =

2. 25 × 62 =

3. 67 × 32 =

4. 75 × 21 =

5. 78 × 42 =

6. 85 × 25 =

7. 92 × 67 =

8. 52 × 28 =

9. 53 × 61 =

10. 65 × 74 =

11. 68 × 51 =

12. 98 × 12 =

13. 63 × 79 =

14. 24 × 23 =

15. 25 × 38 =

16. 45 × 52 =

57

NCTM Standard: Number and Operations – understand ways of representing numbers and work flexibly with positive and negative numbers

Conquer Positive and Negative Numbers

The arrow on the line between each set of numbers represents a whole number and/or a decimal part of the line. Find the whole number or decimal represented by the arrow in the boxes to the right.

1. -2 — +2
2. 0 — +2
3. -2 — -1
4. -3 — -1
5. -5 — -4
6. -5 — -3
7. +3 — +4
8. +4 — +6
9. -6 — -4
10. +4 — +5
11. -7 — -5
12. -6 — -2
13. -20 — -19
14. +19 — +20
15. 0 — +1

+19.5	+4.75	0
+1	-6	+3.25
-5	-4	-3
-4.5	+5	-1.5
-19.5	-2	+0.5

58

NCTM Standard: Number and Operations – understand ways of representing numbers

The arrow on the line between each set of numbers represents a whole number and/or a fraction of the line. Find the whole number and/or fraction represented by the arrow in the boxes to the right.

Mark Some Negative Numbers

-4	-5	-15
$-\frac{1}{4}$	$-3\frac{1}{4}$	$-8\frac{1}{2}$
-1	-6	$-\frac{1}{2}$
$-6\frac{1}{4}$	-2	$-1\frac{1}{4}$
-10	-3	$-1\frac{1}{2}$

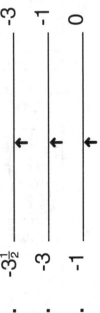
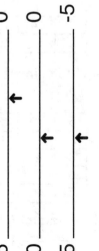

1. $-3\frac{1}{2}$ -3
2. -3   -1
3. -1   0
4. $-1\frac{1}{2}$ -1
5. -6   -2
6. -7   -6
7. $-9\frac{1}{2}$ $-7\frac{1}{2}$
8. -3   0
9. $-\frac{1}{2}$ 0
10. -5   -1
11. -2   0
12. -12   0
13. -15   0
14. -20   0
15. -25   -5

59

Answer Keys

*Only the problem numbers are included in the boxes. It is recommended to write the correct problem numbers on a full-size copy of each math game page to create an answer key.

Hook Some Patterns (p. 3)

7	13	15	3
6	2	12	16
1	8	10	11
5	9	4	14

Nab an Expression (p. 4)

3	15	10	6
4	2	8	12
11	1	13	9
5	7	16	14

Peg Some Algebraic Equations (p. 5)

1	12	6	14
2	8	3	15
5	10	4	13
11	9	16	7

Decimal Dash (p. 6)

8	9	5
4	11	6
7	1	3
12	14	13
15	2	10

Drag in Decimals on a Number Line (p. 7)

6	12	15
13	14	1
3	4	11
8	2	10
5	9	7

Nab a Product (p. 8)

6	1	8	7
3	15	4	16
10	12	11	9
5	14	2	13

Pinch Decimal Multiples (p. 9)

8	16	10	14
4	6	2	9
1	7	3	13
5	15	11	12

Snap Up Change (p. 10)

6	12	4	10
15	1	16	8
7	14	2	11
3	9	13	5

Snare Decimal Multiples (p. 11)

1	7	2	11
15	8	6	12
14	3	16	4
9	10	13	5

A Quotient Sprint (p. 12)

4	13	8	12
10	1	14	6
16	7	2	9
11	3	15	5

Cart Off Some Quotients (p. 13)

6	16	13	1
8	11	9	10
2	15	3	14
12	4	7	5

Grapple for Some Quotients (p. 14)

5	12	9	16
10	3	1	7
15	8	14	2
13	4	11	6

Clip Lowest Common Denominators (p. 15)

16	1	13	6
4	9	12	2
14	3	8	15
7	10	11	5

Conquest Over Common Denominators (p. 16)

3	9	2	4
12	1	16	6
11	7	8	14
5	10	13	15

Find an Improper Fraction (p. 17)

5	11	15	4
3	8	13	7
12	6	1	16
9	2	14	10

Hook Fractions as Part of a Collection (p. 18)

4	8	5	9
14	13	6	16
1	2	7	3
15	12	11	10

Lasso Fractions in a Collection (p. 19)

2	1	8	3
10	4	5	13
12	7	6	9
14	15	11	16

Reduce Those Fractions (p. 20)

11	16	4	8
14	1	9	6
3	15	5	13
7	12	2	10

Snatch the Least Common Multiple (p. 21)

2	5	14
15	3	13
7	11	1
8	4	10
12	6	9

Secure Some Fractions (p. 22)

7	13	1	10
9	2	12	5
3	15	6	14
16	11	4	8

Answer Keys

Snap Up Fractions on a Number Line (p. 23)

6	1	12
13	2	7
3	14	4
8	5	11
10	9	15

Stamp Out Common Denominators (p. 24)

8	12	6
2	7	14
4	1	10
13	5	15
3	11	9

Triumph Over Adding Fractions (p. 25)

6	16	10	2
3	1	11	15
5	7	4	8
14	12	13	9

Button Down Fractions and Decimals (p. 26)

11	7	9
4	8	2
5	1	12
15	10	6
13	3	14

Collar Some Multiples (p. 27)

13	6	16	4
5	3	11	9
8	12	10	14
1	15	2	7

Salvage Lots of Percent Equivalents (p. 28)

9	6	13	11
7	16	3	2
12	1	15	8
4	10	5	14

Strike Out Some Mixed Numbers (p. 29)

8	10	23	4	13
24	1	17	9	20
5	18	2	21	14
12	19	3	16	7
25	6	22	11	15

Pounce on a Percent (p. 30)

7	12	11	4
2	16	1	14
9	3	15	8
10	6	13	5

Round Up Percents (p. 31)

9	1	10
5	14	4
12	3	8
13	15	11
2	6	7

Bag Some Huge Numbers (p. 32)

1	12	4
10	3	15
5	14	6
11	2	13
7	9	8

Bring in Some Big Numbers (p. 33)

11	2	13	8
3	9	16	6
4	7	1	14
10	15	5	12

Grab Base Ten Number Representations (p. 34)

11	4	13	6
2	1	12	7
16	10	3	15
8	9	14	5

Pull in Some Place Value (p. 35)

14	8	15
1	2	9
7	10	6
12	3	13
4	5	11

Draw in Ratios (p. 36)

10	8	6
9	1	14
13	3	2
4	11	5
15	7	12

Rack Up Ratios (p. 37)

13	9	5
11	14	8
7	2	12
3	10	4
15	1	6

Drag in Addition Estimation Answers (p. 38)

13	7	11
2	15	3
12	1	6
4	9	8
10	14	5

Rope Some Averages (p. 39)

6	16	2	12
7	1	11	8
4	13	3	14
10	9	15	5

Peg Subtraction Answers (p. 40)

1	9	14	8
7	13	4	12
11	2	10	5
6	16	3	15

Button Down the Cummutative Property (p. 41)

2	3	10
8	5	13
9	11	6
14	7	4
15	1	12

Answer Keys

Latch Onto Square Root Estimations (p. 42)

14	6	1
8	9	12
4	2	7
11	3	13
10	15	5

Overcome Exponents (p. 43)

14	1	3	12
6	13	10	4
7	11	5	16
8	2	15	9

Crunch the Area of Triangles (p. 44)

4	16	6	11
8	1	15	2
13	12	3	10
9	5	14	7

Conquer Geometric Shapes (p. 45)

3	13	12
5	4	9
14	7	2
6	11	10
1	8	15

Latch Onto Areas (p. 46)

8	6	11
2	4	9
10	7	1
12	5	3

Master Coordinates (p. 47)

5	13	15	11
19	4	6	14
1	16	2	17
3	8	7	20
10	9	12	18

Nab a Coordinate (p. 48)

C	J	N
F	H	B
A	K	M
E	I	G
L	O	D

Play With Perimeters (p. 49)

10	8	4
3	1	7
6	11	12
5	9	2

Reach for Rectangular Areas (p. 50)

4	8	5
7	2	15
10	3	11
9	6	14
12	13	1

Snatch Geometric Patterns (p. 51)

12	2	14	16
4	1	15	10
6	7	3	11
8	5	9	13

Stamp Out Surface Areas (p. 52)

8	11	3
6	1	14
2	15	12
4	13	7
10	5	9

Crunch Customary Units (p. 53)

11	1	7	8
5	12	4	13
3	6	10	2
16	15	9	14

Tackle Metric Measurement (p. 54)

13	14	3	5
6	8	10	4
16	1	12	7
11	15	2	9

Grasp the Inverse Operation (p. 55)

11	8	2	5
13	4	15	1
12	9	7	10
3	14	6	16

Haul in Some Inverse Operations (p. 56)

7	12	2	9
3	1	6	8
13	4	5	16
11	14	15	10

Snag a Big Multiple (p. 57)

2	4	6	8
15	12	1	5
7	11	16	10
3	9	13	14

Conquer Positive and Negative Numbers (p. 58)

14	10	1
2	11	7
9	6	12
5	8	3
13	4	15

Mark Some Negative Numbers (p. 59)

5	13	15
9	1	7
11	12	3
6	2	4
14	10	8